THINGS THAT GO

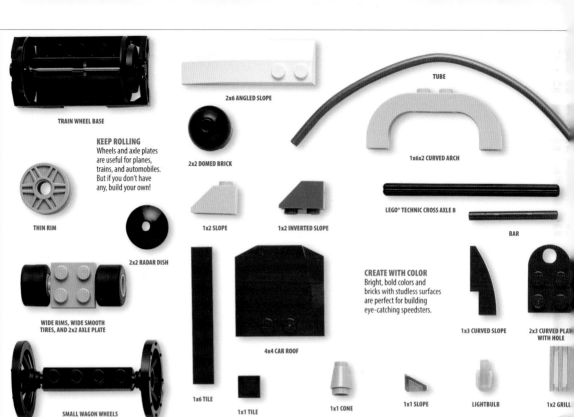

TRAIN WHEEL BASE

2x6 ANGLED SLOPE

TUBE

1x6x2 CURVED ARCH

KEEP ROLLING
Wheels and axle plates are useful for planes, trains, and automobiles. But if you don't have any, build your own!

2x2 DOMED BRICK

LEGO® TECHNIC CROSS AXLE 8

THIN RIM

1x2 SLOPE

1x2 INVERTED SLOPE

BAR

2x2 RADAR DISH

CREATE WITH COLOR
Bright, bold colors and bricks with studless surfaces are perfect for building eye-catching speedsters.

WIDE RIMS, WIDE SMOOTH TIRES, AND 2x2 AXLE PLATE

4x4 CAR ROOF

1x3 CURVED SLOPE

2x3 CURVED PLATE WITH HOLE

SMALL WAGON WHEELS AND 1x4 AXLE PLATE

1x6 TILE

1x1 TILE

1x1 CONE

1x1 SLOPE

LIGHTBULB

1x2 GRILL

SMOOTH PIECES
Use tiles and other smooth pieces to give your vehicles a sleek, aerodynamic look.

2x2 PLATE WITH DOUBLE WHEEL

1x2 PRINTED TILE

LIGHT 'EM UP
Transparent pieces make great headlights, taillights, navigation lights—even spotlights!

1x1 ROUND PLATE

1x2 PRINTED TILE

1x1 ROUND PLATE

LEGO TECHNIC RIM AND BALLOON TIRE

THIN TREAD TIRE

WHEEL RIM AND TIRE

STEERING WHEEL

SEAT

2x2 PRINTED ROUND TILE

JOYSTICK

START UP YOUR ENGINES

To build amazing transport vehicles you'll need all the basics—wheels, axles, propellers. But don't just stick to LEGO® car or airplane sets! Look through your entire collection and choose some really exciting pieces to give your models an unusual shape or imaginative detail. Here are some good bricks to look out for.

BARRED WINDOW WITH 4 CONNECTIONS

1x2 GRILLE SLOPE

**RICK WITH
DE STUD**

**1x2 PLATE WITH
VERTICAL BAR**

1x2/1x4 ANGLE PLATE

ANGLE PLATES
Angle plates are great
for attaching grilles and
lights to the front or back
of your model.

1x2/2x2 ANGLE PLATE

1x1 PLATE WITH SIDE RING

**2x2 BRICK WITH SIDE
PINS AND AXLE HOLE**

**PLATE WITH
TICAL CLIP**

**1x1 BRICK WITH
VERTICAL BAR**

**1x2 HINGED BRICK AND
1x2 HINGED PLATE**

HINGED PLATES

1x1 HEADLIGHT BRICK

1x2 PLATE WITH HANDLED BAR

SKELETON ARM

**1x2 PLATE WITH
LEGO TECHNIC BEAM**

**1x2
UMPER
PLATE**

**1x2 PLATE WITH
HANDLED BAR**

1x2 CURVED HALF ARCH

LEGO TECHNIC T-BAR

CHOOSE BRICKS
FROM ACROSS ALL YOUR
LEGO SETS TO BUILD
UNIQUE VEHICLES

2x2 TURNTABLE

1x2 TEXTURED BRICK

TRAIN BUFFER

**1x1 PLATE WITH
HORIZONTAL CLIP**

**LEGO TECHNIC
HALF PIN**

**LEGO TECHNIC
HALF BUSH**

2x2 TILE WITH PIN

2x4 WHEEL GUARD

WHEEL GUARDS
Ready-made wheel guard pieces
can help construct the base of your
model. Choose printed pieces to
add detail! (See Hot Rod, p.7)

**PROPELLER
WITH 4 BLADES**

1x2x2 LADDER

1x2 PLATE WITH SIDE BARS

2x4 WINGED WHEEL GUARD

2x2 BRICK WITH WHEEL ARCH

NEW PURPOSE
Try to think of exciting
new uses for your
pieces. This webbed
radar dish (below)
makes a great propeller!
(See Swampboat, p.15)

2x4 WHEEL GUARD

**2x2 PLATE WITH
FRONT GRILLE**

1x6 CURVED BAR WITH STUDS

**PROPELLER
WITH 3 BLADES**

A CLEAR PLACE TO START
Windshields and windows
are a good starting point
for a vehicle. They can
help determine the size
of your model.

**1x2x2
WALL ELEMENT**

LEGO TECHNIC WIDE RIM

6x6 WEBBED RADAR DISH

CURVED WINDSHIELD

**1x4x3 WINDOW FRAME
WITH WINDOW GLASS**

2x4x2 WINDSHIELD

CARS

It's time to hit the road! Before building a car, think about where you're going. For city driving, you could make a compact auto to fit a single minifigure. For off-road vehicles, add some rugged, outdoor features. Whatever you build, make sure the driver fits inside and the wheels can spin freely!

DOORLESS ENTRY

Doors can be tricky to build, but even if you leave doors out, you can still make a handle using a headlight brick and a 1x1 tile. You could make a removable gas cap, too!

BUILDING BRIEF

Objective: Create small automobiles
Use: Personal travel, transportation
Features: Four wheels, windshield, headlights, steering wheel
Extras: Roof rack, spare tire, trunk space, additional seats

Roof pops off to let driver in and out

Hood ornament on 1-stud jumper plate

Same piece for front and rear windshields

REAR VIEW

License plate. You could also use a printed tile

Side mirror, made from plate with side ring. You could attach a 1x1 slope, plate, or tile, instead

Taillights—transparent tiles built into body of car can be any color

CITY CAR

To navigate the narrow streets of a bustling city, design a compact car. Build the basic shell first, and then add details like a front grille, headlights, and license plate.

WISH I COULD FEEL THE BREEZE THROUGH MY HAIR...BUT IT'S PLASTIC!

Take off roof and rear windshield to make a convertible!

1x1/2x2 angle plate

AUTO ANATOMY

This car was built on a base of overlapping rectangular plates with axle plates underneath to attach the wheels. The front details are mounted on an angle plate.

UNDER THE HOOD

The front is held together by an assembly of bricks, clips, and sideways building. When you build in multiple directions, the more points of contact you have, and the better it holds together.

CARGO SPACE

This car has front and back seats and a small trunk to store anything your minifigure might need on the road. You could take out the rear seats to make a larger trunk.

Roof lights for foggy nights. Use transparent red pieces for hi-tech night vision!

Pack a spare tire for emergencies on the back or in the trunk

1x1 slopes mirror shape of front of roof

OFF-ROAD CAR

For a more complex car, create something with a special purpose, like driving across rough terrain! This auto was built from the top down, with the roof, hood, and windshield pieces picked out first and then the rest constructed to fit them.

Put transparent slopes on their side for a different effect

Brick-built wheel guards. Make sure the tires have clearance to turn!

Use different color bricks in the car's body to add decoration, stripes, dirt, or camouflage

MONSTER TRUCKS

Who says that cars and trucks have to be down-to-earth? With a few special pieces and lots of imagination, you can turn your creation into the craziest car around. From towering turbo trucks to super-fast speedsters, these over-amped autos rule the road, the ring, and the racetrack!

BUILDING BRIEF

Objective: Build souped-up muscle vehicles
Use: Competition, racing, showing off!
Features: Everything a normal vehicle has, but to the extreme!
Extras: Giant wheels, big exhausts, spikes, chains, flames, fins, spoilers

LEGO Technic half beam

Elastic band

IN SUSPENSE

To make the springy suspension, the wheels are attached to pivoting LEGO Technic half beams. Elastic bands pull the beams toward the center, so when a wheel is pushed out of position, it springs right back in again.

Boosters made from wheel rims—or use jet engines to go even more over the top!

REAR SIDE VIEW

SKELETON TURBO

Don't let the cheery yellow fool you—this monster means business! It is built around a working suspension system that lets each oversized wheel move independently to conquer or crush any obstacle in its path.

Rollcage built with clips and robot claws

Build a row of bars to clip on mirrors, chains, and spikes

Chunky grille made from barred window

Use curved and bumpy pieces as debris to test suspension

Vented engine made from 1x1 round plates

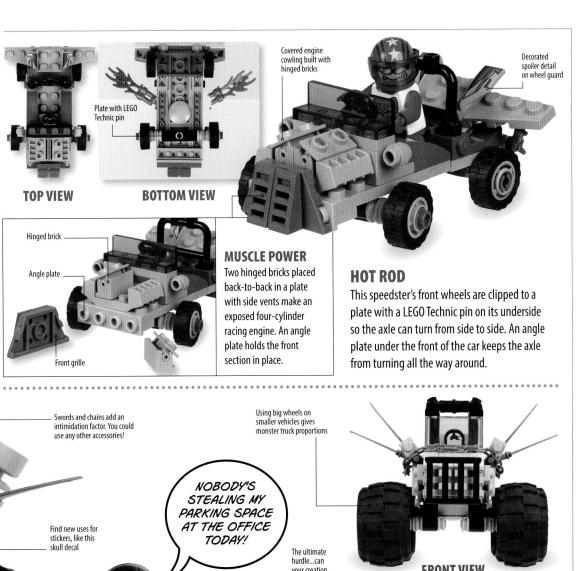

TOP VIEW

BOTTOM VIEW

Plate with LEGO Technic pin

Covered engine cowling built with hinged bricks

Decorated spoiler detail on wheel guard

Hinged brick

Angle plate

Front grille

MUSCLE POWER

Two hinged bricks placed back-to-back in a plate with side vents make an exposed four-cylinder racing engine. An angle plate holds the front section in place.

HOT ROD

This speedster's front wheels are clipped to a plate with a LEGO Technic pin on its underside so the axle can turn from side to side. An angle plate under the front of the car keeps the axle from turning all the way around.

Swords and chains add an intimidation factor. You could use any other accessories!

Using big wheels on smaller vehicles gives monster truck proportions

Find new uses for stickers, like this skull decal

NOBODY'S STEALING MY PARKING SPACE AT THE OFFICE TODAY!

The ultimate hurdle...can your creation overcome it?

FRONT VIEW

REAR VIEW

TRUCKS

Big trucks, little trucks, construction trucks, farm trucks, highway trucks with box trailers, fuel tanker trucks, and postal delivery trucks—as long as it has wheels and carries cargo, it's a truck. They might drive cross-country or work at the docks, they might have four wheels or eighteen, but if you have the pieces, you can build them!

BUILDING BRIEF
Objective: Build trucks
Use: Hauling all kinds of loads
Features: Wheels, strength, size, cargo space
Extras: More wheels, moving functions, detachable trailer

TRANSPORT TRUCK

A truck doesn't have to be big to be packed with details. Gray, brown, and tan bricks make this classic hauler look well-worn and rustic. It may be carrying cabbages now, but its wooden-slat bed can haul just about anything!

FACING FORWARD

The front grille, headlights, and other details are built onto a plate and then connected to the rest of the truck using an angle plate.

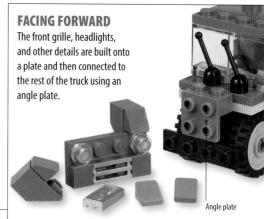

Angle plate

Wooden cargo bed made with stacked headlight bricks and long tiles

Slopes create an angled front

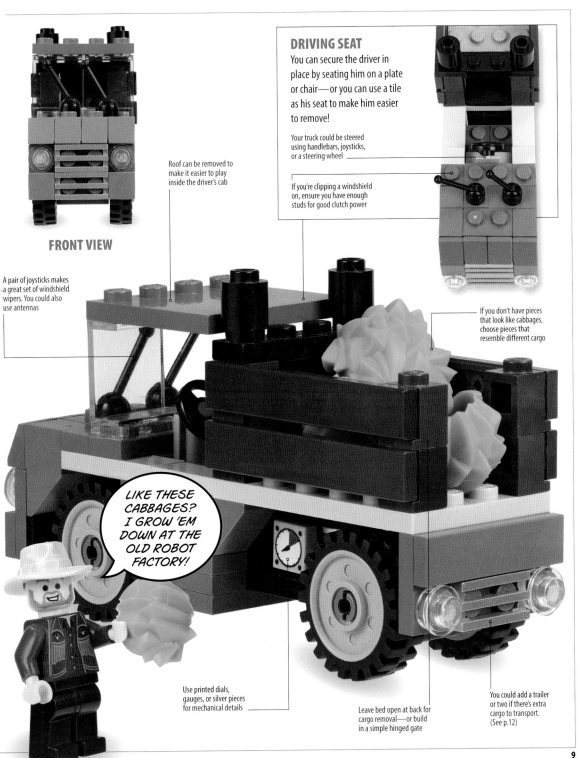

FRONT VIEW

DRIVING SEAT

You can secure the driver in place by seating him on a plate or chair—or you can use a tile as his seat to make him easier to remove!

Your truck could be steered using handlebars, joysticks, or a steering wheel

If you're clipping a windshield on, ensure you have enough studs for good clutch power

Roof can be removed to make it easier to play inside the driver's cab

A pair of joysticks makes a great set of windshield wipers. You could also use antennas

If you don't have pieces that look like cabbages, choose pieces that resemble different cargo

LIKE THESE CABBAGES? I GROW 'EM DOWN AT THE OLD ROBOT FACTORY!

Use printed dials, gauges, or silver pieces for mechanical details

Leave bed open at back for cargo removal—or build in a simple hinged gate

You could add a trailer or two if there's extra cargo to transport. (See p.12)

ICE CREAM TRUCK

On a hot summer's day, the sight of a friendly ice cream truck is always welcome! Make your truck festive and colorful with decorative pieces. Don't forget to stock the back with plenty of frozen treats so you can serve all your customers some tasty ice cream!

BUILDING BRIEF
Objective: Make ice cream trucks
Use: Transportation, selling treats
Features: Window, removable roof
Extras: Goblets, pieces to personalize your truck

CHOOSE YOUR FLAVOR

The ice cream truck has an iconic shape. Use curved half arches at the front of the truck to achieve this look. Add tiles to the top of the roof to make it smooth, but don't worry if you don't have enough tiles; exposed studs are okay, too.

BOTTOM VIEW

Flower pieces brighten up truck

MAIN ATTRACTION

To attract potential customers, make your truck eye-catching! You could attach flowers or other accessories to the side of your truck with a headlight brick. Colored round plates could look like scoops of ice cream.

Roof made from plates topped with tiles

Air vent keeps the inside of your truck cool

Printed scroll pieces make great menus. What's on offer today?

MY ICE CREAMS ARE SPECIAL. WHY? THEY DON'T MELT!

Built-in window as serving hatch

Red wheel arches match the red roof. You could use your favorite colors

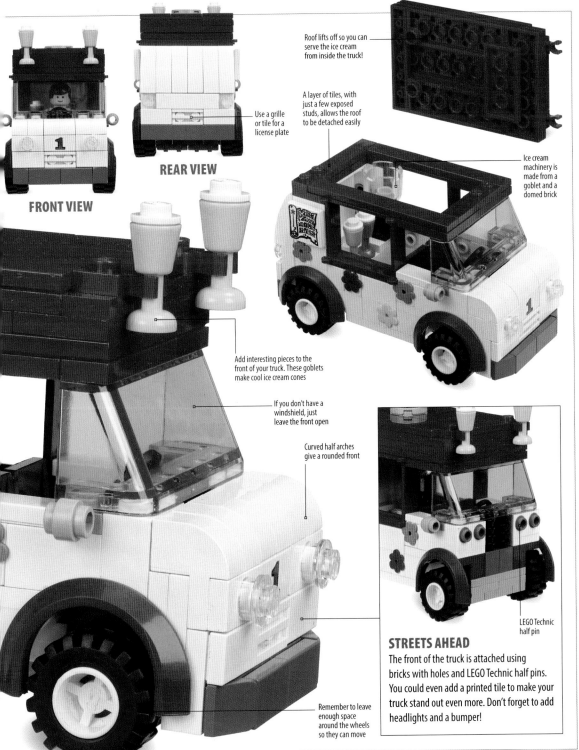

FRONT VIEW

REAR VIEW

Use a grille or tile for a license plate

Roof lifts off so you can serve the ice cream from inside the truck!

A layer of tiles, with just a few exposed studs, allows the roof to be detached easily

Ice cream machinery is made from a goblet and a domed brick

Add interesting pieces to the front of your truck. These goblets make cool ice cream cones

If you don't have a windshield, just leave the front open

Curved half arches give a rounded front

LEGO Technic half pin

Remember to leave enough space around the wheels so they can move

STREETS AHEAD

The front of the truck is attached using bricks with holes and LEGO Technic half pins. You could even add a printed tile to make your truck stand out even more. Don't forget to add headlights and a bumper!

SMALL VEHICLES

They're bigger than bicycles but smaller than cars! Small vehicles serve all kinds of purposes for all sorts of drivers, from navigating across bumpy terrain to cruising over a golf course. They can park in small spaces, pass through narrow gaps, and fit inside your pocket. Here are some ideas to get you started!

BUILDING BRIEF
Objective: Build small vehicles
Use: Movement, transport
Features: Wheels, handles, controls
Extras: Trailers, transport trucks, tiny garages

IF YOU'RE GOING TO GO EXPLORING, DON'T FORGET YOUR HAT!

Ears of corn—what else can you transport?

Grille attached with minifigure angle plate

Angle plate holds taillights and license plate in place

Brown bars makes the front grille look chunky and hard-wearing

QUAD BIKE

Take your adventures off-road by building an all-terrain vehicle with a compact, tough shape and four big wheels. Add an easy-to-attach trailer for special expeditions!

Standing driver has good control of the vehicle, but you could make it a seated vehicle

Make sure wheel guards are raised enough so wheels can turn

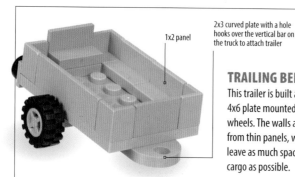

1x2 panel

2x3 curved plate with a hole hooks over the vertical bar on the truck to attach trailer

TRAILING BEHIND

This trailer is built around a 4x6 plate mounted on two wheels. The walls are made from thin panels, which leave as much space for cargo as possible.

1x2 plate with vertical bar attaches trailer

REAR SIDE VIEW

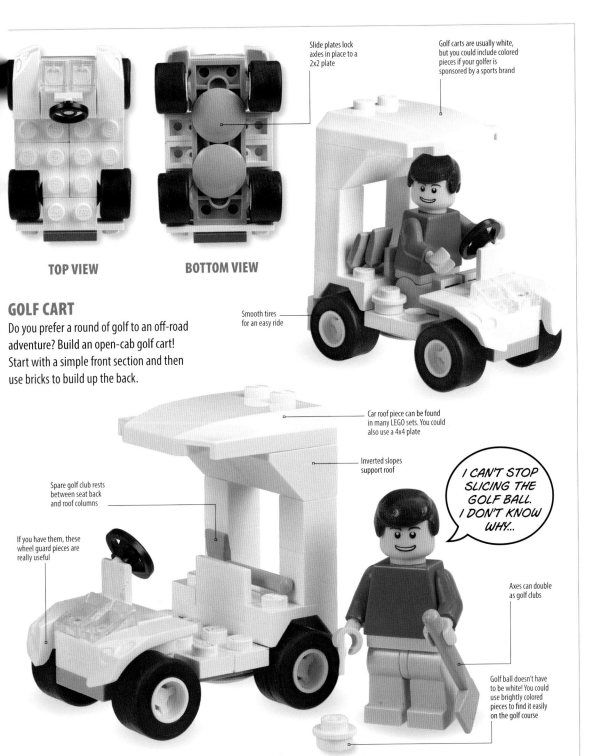

TOP VIEW

BOTTOM VIEW

Slide plates lock axles in place to a 2x2 plate

Golf carts are usually white, but you could include colored pieces if your golfer is sponsored by a sports brand

Smooth tires for an easy ride

GOLF CART

Do you prefer a round of golf to an off-road adventure? Build an open-cab golf cart! Start with a simple front section and then use bricks to build up the back.

Car roof piece can be found in many LEGO sets. You could also use a 4x4 plate

Inverted slopes support roof

Spare golf club rests between seat back and roof columns

If you have them, these wheel guard pieces are really useful

I CAN'T STOP SLICING THE GOLF BALL. I DON'T KNOW WHY...

Axes can double as golf clubs

Golf ball doesn't have to be white! You could use brightly colored pieces to find it easily on the golf course

13

AROUND THE WORLD

From the rickshaws of Asia and the gondolas of Italy to the swampboats of the Florida Everglades, the world is chock full of transport vehicles designed to navigate different environments and terrains. What other exotic forms of transport can you think of? Look out for ideas on your next vacation!

BUILDING BRIEF
Objective: Build international transport vehicles
Use: Carrying a driver and passengers
Features: All kinds of form and propulsion
Extras: Environments, local buildings, landmarks

HURRY UP! I'VE GOT A GONDOLA TO CATCH.

THIS JOB MAY NOT PAY MUCH, BUT IT'S GREAT EXERCISE.

Ski pole holds up the roof

RICKSHAW

The base of this foot-powered rickshaw is built on its side, so the bars and wheels can be attached. Make sure the canopy is positioned high enough so that the minifigure passenger can fit in.

Wheels similar to wagon wheels are often used on rickshaws, even today

Make sure the bars are the right width apart that the driver can hold them both at the same time!

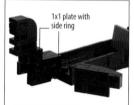

1x1 plate with side ring

Raised prow built with a headlight brick, a stack of plates, a curved half arch, and a tile

BOAT BRICKS

Two plates with a side ring hold the curved sides together at the front of the gondola. One of them also attaches the curved sections to the main body of the boat.

GONDOLA

This flat-bottomed Venetian boat combines normal brick stacking with sideways building to create a curved, narrow outline. An angle plate gives the gondolier a set of studs to stand on.

A dapper tourist always packs a tuxedo!

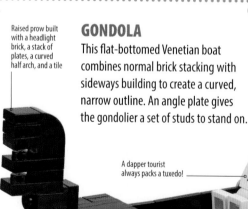

Long oar made from ski pole combined with umbrella pole

SWAMPBOAT

This model started with a great idea for using a big webbed radar dish. Add a propeller, an engine piece, a platform, and some floats, and you've got a good old-fashioned swamp-cruiser!

Webbed radar dish

1x2 plate with handled bar

Don't have bars for a railing? Build a barrier out of bricks and tiles instead!

FLOAT BUILDING

Twin catamaran floats are built upside-down using two pairs of angled slopes. They are attached to the main platform using plates with handled bars.

Streamer adds height and color to model

Tube railing held in place by skeleton legs

Connect propeller with a LEGO Technic pin so it can really spin!

GOOD THING ALLIGATORS CAN'T CLIMB... CAN THEY?

Big floats raise driver platform above hungry alligators

Engine casings and vent built from curved half arches and a printed tile

CLASSIC TRAINS

To build an old-style train, you don't need a lot of special parts! Find some pictures of steam trains for reference and choose the perfect pieces from your LEGO collection. Then, get building—all you need is a little loco-motivation!

BUILDING BRIEF
Objective: Build classic steam trains
Use: Rail-based transport of passengers and cargo
Features: Wheels, smokestack, furnace, engineer
Extras: Freight cars, passenger cars, coal wagon, rails

STEAM ENGINE

The key to building a steam locomotive is capturing the shape of the classic train engine: a cylinder with a smokestack in front, a box for the engineer's cabin, and wheels underneath.

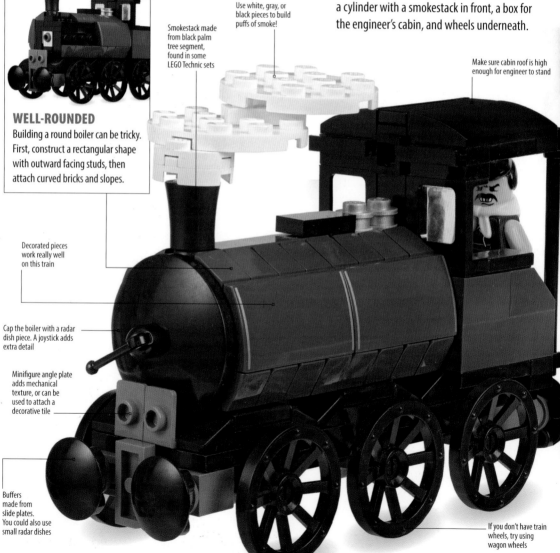

WELL-ROUNDED

Building a round boiler can be tricky. First, construct a rectangular shape with outward facing studs, then attach curved bricks and slopes.

Smokestack made from black palm tree segment, found in some LEGO Technic sets

Use white, gray, or black pieces to build puffs of smoke!

Make sure cabin roof is high enough for engineer to stand

Decorated pieces work really well on this train

Cap the boiler with a radar dish piece. A joystick adds extra detail

Minifigure angle plate adds mechanical texture, or can be used to attach a decorative tile

Buffers made from slide plates. You could also use small radar dishes

If you don't have train wheels, try using wagon wheels

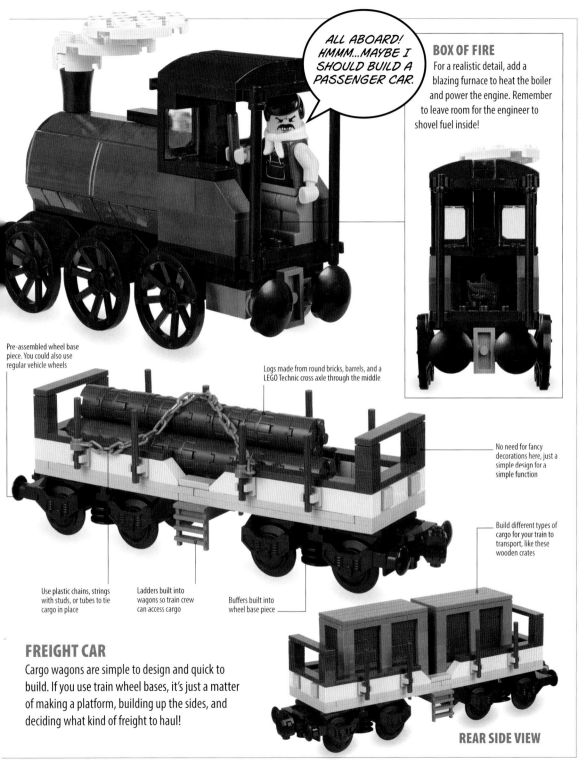

ALL ABOARD! HMMM...MAYBE I SHOULD BUILD A PASSENGER CAR.

BOX OF FIRE

For a realistic detail, add a blazing furnace to heat the boiler and power the engine. Remember to leave room for the engineer to shovel fuel inside!

Pre-assembled wheel base piece. You could also use regular vehicle wheels

Logs made from round bricks, barrels, and a LEGO Technic cross axle through the middle

No need for fancy decorations here, just a simple design for a simple function

Build different types of cargo for your train to transport, like these wooden crates

Use plastic chains, strings with studs, or tubes to tie cargo in place

Ladders built into wagons so train crew can access cargo

Buffers built into wheel base piece

FREIGHT CAR

Cargo wagons are simple to design and quick to build. If you use train wheel bases, it's just a matter of making a platform, building up the sides, and deciding what kind of freight to haul!

REAR SIDE VIEW

CITY TRAINS

Trains run through many modern cities, from above-ground commuter lines to subways in tunnels beneath the streets. They are built for speed and efficiency, so they usually have a compact, tube-shaped profile. Match the colors of your favorite city's trains or try building a super-streamlined bullet express!

BUILDING BRIEF
Objective: Build modern city trains
Use: Urban transportation, commuting
Features: Boxy shape, multiple doors, plenty of sitting and standing room
Extras: Bogies, passengers, tunnels, station platforms, rain shelters

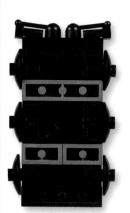

BOTTOM VIEW

Wheels are made using radar dish pieces held on by LEGO Technic half pins. Can you think of a way to make them rotate?

BUILD-A-BOGIE

The wheeled undercarriage seen on modern trains is known as a bogie. If you don't have train pieces, try making a bogie using LEGO Technic half pins, radar dishes, and tiles. You can even link train cars together by adding ball-and-socket joints or plates with vertical bars and holes.

Turntable lets the section swivel, but keeps the wheels lined up as it goes around curves

LEGO Technic half pin

Joysticks, binoculars, or antennas can represent braking pins and beams

OPEN-TOP TRAIN

The sections of roof between the doors can be removed easily for quick access to the train's interior.

Curved slopes are perfect to get the shape of this train

Vertical hand rails are a common feature of subway trains

SUBWAY TRAIN

This subway train is designed to travel smoothly underground. The distinctive roof is built from curved slopes, with transparent slopes used at the top of the doors.

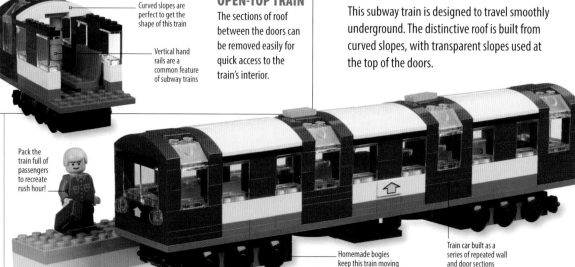

Pack the train full of passengers to recreate rush hour!

Homemade bogies keep this train moving

Train car built as a series of repeated wall and door sections

MIND THE GAP

The windshield is built onto hinged bricks and plates, which creates a sloping angle at the front of the trolley car. The gaps on either side are hidden by tall slopes.

Tall slope

Hinged brick

Door handles made from plates with side rings

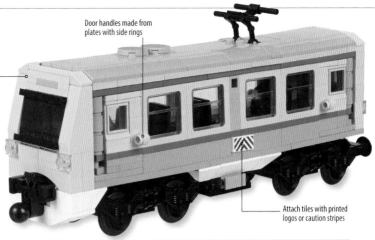

Attach tiles with printed logos or caution stripes

POWER SOURCE

Above-ground trains use roof-mounted devices to collect electricity from overhead power lines. It's easy to build one—you just need some bar pieces and robot or skeleton arms!

Create doors in a different color so they stand out from rest of car

1x1 plate with horizontal clip

Round bricks give door room to swing open

...ick with ...ll joint

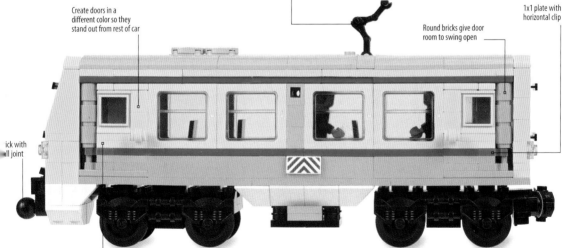

ALL ABOARD!

The doors of the train open and close, thanks to two plates with horizontal clips that are built into each door. The clips attach to a vertical bar, which acts as a hinge. You could also use hinged plates or bricks.

ABOVE-GROUND TRAIN

This overground train is built on six-stud-wide plates and rolls on wheel base pieces. Cars can be connected with ball-and-socket joints, so your train can follow curves in the track!

AIRPLANES

There's a whole sky full of airplanes for you to build!
You can make a vintage plane with an open cockpit, an
ultra-modern passenger jet, or anything in between.
Big planes, little planes, biplanes, triplanes—even cargo
planes with loading ramps and space inside to carry your
auto models. Grab your bricks and prepare for take-off!

BUILDING BRIEF
Objective: Make airplanes
Use: Travel through the air
Features: Wings, cockpit, engines
or propellers, tailfins, landing gear
Extras: Passenger or cargo space,
extra wings or engines, ejector seats
with parachutes

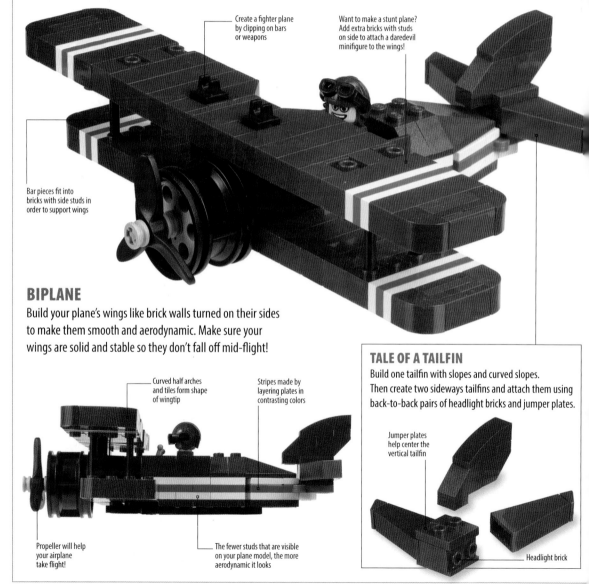

Create a fighter plane
by clipping on bars
or weapons

Want to make a stunt plane?
Add extra bricks with studs
on side to attach a daredevil
minifigure to the wings!

Bar pieces fit into
bricks with side studs in
order to support wings

BIPLANE

Build your plane's wings like brick walls turned on their sides
to make them smooth and aerodynamic. Make sure your
wings are solid and stable so they don't fall off mid-flight!

Curved half arches
and tiles form shape
of wingtip

Stripes made by
layering plates in
contrasting colors

Propeller will help
your airplane
take flight!

The fewer studs that are visible
on your plane model, the more
aerodynamic it looks

TALE OF A TAILFIN

Build one tailfin with slopes and curved slopes.
Then create two sideways tailfins and attach them using
back-to-back pairs of headlight bricks and jumper plates.

Jumper plates
help center the
vertical tailfin

Headlight brick

MICROPLANE

You don't need to build a big model to make a big plane. Microscale airplanes are easy to create and look great. Just make sure you include the key features that make your plane recognizable!

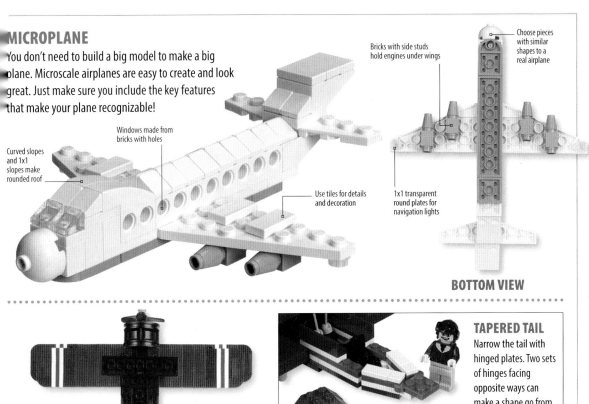

Choose pieces with similar shapes to a real airplane

Bricks with side studs hold engines under wings

Windows made from bricks with holes

Curved slopes and 1x1 slopes make rounded roof

Use tiles for details and decoration

1x1 transparent round plates for navigation lights

BOTTOM VIEW

TAPERED TAIL
Narrow the tail with hinged plates. Two sets of hinges facing opposite ways can make a shape go from straight to angled to straight again.

Plates at bottom lock plane body together

BOTTOM VIEW

TRIPLANE

Use the bricks with side studs on the top wing to convert a biplane into a triplane!

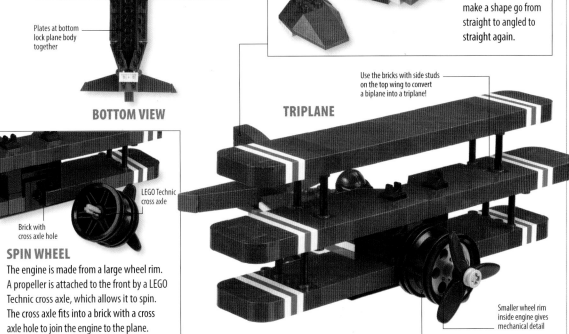

LEGO Technic cross axle

Brick with cross axle hole

SPIN WHEEL
The engine is made from a large wheel rim. A propeller is attached to the front by a LEGO Technic cross axle, which allows it to spin. The cross axle fits into a brick with a cross axle hole to join the engine to the plane.

Smaller wheel rim inside engine gives mechanical detail

HOT AIR BALLOON

The most important thing to remember about a hot air balloon is its shape. You may think of a balloon as a sphere, but it's really more like a lightbulb shape. The second most important thing is stability: round shapes need lots of bricks, so make sure they're all locked together securely!

BRICK BALLOON

Build a balloon shape one layer at a time, starting at the bottom and building upward. Overlap the bricks to keep the outline as round as possible. The basket is made from a plate built up with rows of bricks, plates, and tiles.

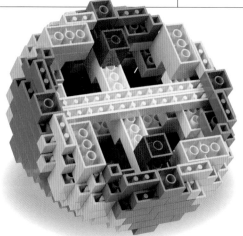

HEAVIER THAN AIR

Build your balloon from the bottom up, gradually stepping outward and then sharply inward toward the top. To cut down the weight, make the balloon's center hollow and strengthen it with crossed bricks inside.

Make a swirl by moving the colors one stud over on each new layer

Add a burner flame to keep the balloon aloft

Ballast sacks made from plates with vertical clips on blank minifigure heads

WAIT...HOW DO I GET BACK DOWN AGAIN?

Long LEGO Technic cross axles attach basket to balloon

1x1 round bricks are good for a wicker texture

HELICOPTER

Helicopters come in all shapes and sizes, and are designed for lots of different jobs. Decide what kind you want to make before you start building: A lightweight news chopper with a camera? A rescue copter with lots of cargo space? Big helicopters can have multiple rotors on top to keep them flying high!

BUILDING BRIEF
Objective: Create helicopters
Use: Controlled hovering flight, transport
Features: Top rotor, tail rotor, cockpit, skids, landing gear
Extras: Cameras, rescue equipment, additional rotors

Boosters or rockets can be held together with a bar or antenna through the middle

Intakes built from harpoons inserted into radar dishes, round bricks, and domed bricks

RESCUE COPTER

This emergency chopper's bright color makes it easy to spot out at sea. Its body is built thinner and thinner toward the tail, tapering from six studs wide to only two.

Add small tools and weapons to equip your chopper for rescue!

Big window shutters make an easy-to-open cargo hatch

LEGO Technic half pin

Use pieces with interesting shapes, like this car roof

SIDE VIEW

To shape the side of your helicopter, use 1x2 bricks with holes with LEGO Technic half pins in them to secure angled pieces. Windows and slopes add detail, too.

Swap intakes for round transparent plates to make spotlights for nighttime rescues!

Row of 1x1 slopes creates a sleek angled side

Unusual pieces like telescopes and steering wheels used as rescue equipment

COPTER COMPONENTS

Choose your windshield first and use that as a guide for the helicopter's dimensions. A spacious cockpit with side windows gives your crew a wide view for spotting trouble.

BOATS

What kind of boat do you want to build? Whether you'd prefer a pocket-sized microship or a minifigure-scale vessel with a detailed interior, here are some maritime models to get you started. Build a speedboat for zipping around the bay, or a luxury cruise liner for sailing the seas—just don't forget to give your masterpiece a name!

BUILDING BRIEF
Objective: Create ships and boats
Use: Marine travel, transportation
Features: Strong hull, smokestacks, propellers
Extras: Life preservers, crew cabins, cargo hold

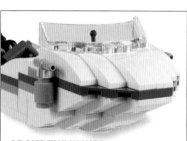

ABOVE THE WAVES
Use two layers of inverted slopes on the bottom of the prow and a layer of curved slopes on top for a streamlined shape!

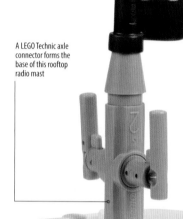

A LEGO Technic axle connector forms the base of this rooftop radio mast

SPEEDBOAT
This flashy boat's main body is built from white plates, with a tan floor for color contrast. Blue plates create a wave pattern for a really aquatic look! The cabin roof can be removed, with 1x1 slopes filling the gaps left by the support columns.

Hinged brick and plate allows motor to tilt up and down

Push a T-bar into a round brick for a clip-on float

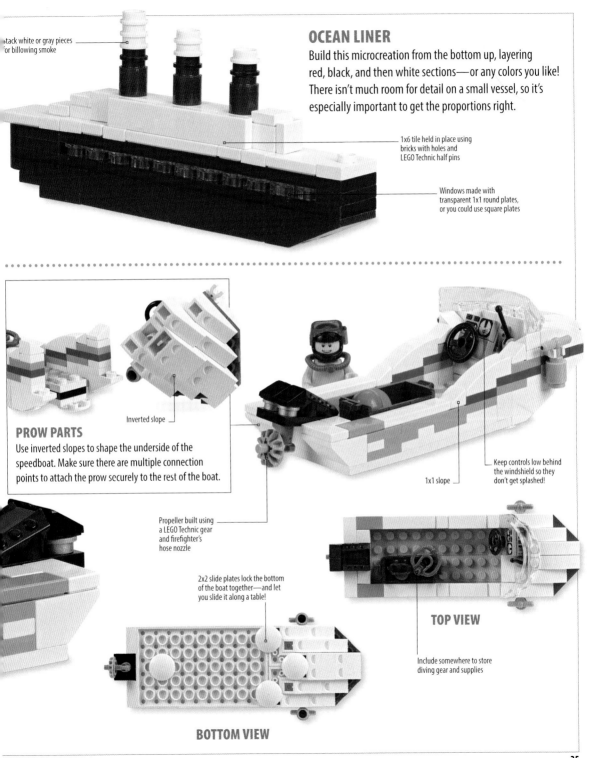

Stack white or gray pieces for billowing smoke

OCEAN LINER

Build this microcreation from the bottom up, layering red, black, and then white sections—or any colors you like! There isn't much room for detail on a small vessel, so it's especially important to get the proportions right.

1x6 tile held in place using bricks with holes and LEGO Technic half pins

Windows made with transparent 1x1 round plates, or you could use square plates

Inverted slope

PROW PARTS

Use inverted slopes to shape the underside of the speedboat. Make sure there are multiple connection points to attach the prow securely to the rest of the boat.

Keep controls low behind the windshield so they don't get splashed!

1x1 slope

Propeller built using a LEGO Technic gear and firefighter's hose nozzle

2x2 slide plates lock the bottom of the boat together—and let you slide it along a table!

TOP VIEW

Include somewhere to store diving gear and supplies

BOTTOM VIEW

FISHING BOAT

You don't need lots of special pieces to build a fishing boat. You can create the perfect seafaring vessel with some of your own bricks and plenty of imagination. Start with the hull and a cabin, then add nautical details like rigging, anchors, and radio equipment. You don't even need to build a whole boat—just build the part that floats above the waves!

Objective: Build fishing boats
Use: Catching fish out at sea
Features: Strong hull, nets, control room, crew
Extras: Warning lights, tracking gear, lifeboats, cranes, fishing nets

GONE FISHING

The toughest part of making a boat without specialized hull pieces is getting the shape right. This model uses hinged pieces to make the shape for the hull, and has lots of improvised building. The front mast was originally the center of a spiral staircase!

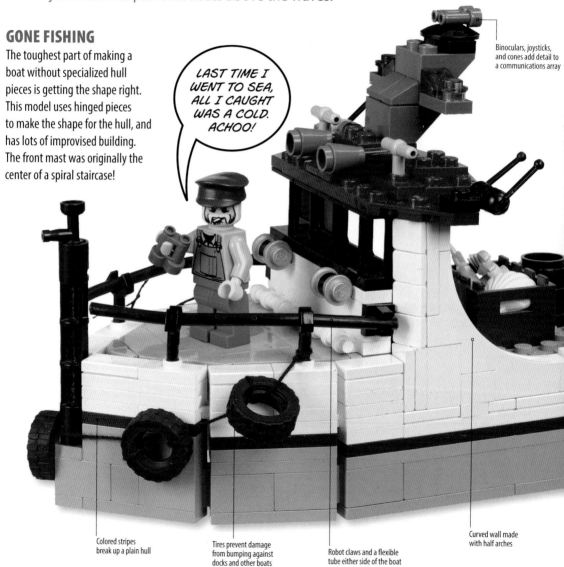

LAST TIME I WENT TO SEA, ALL I CAUGHT WAS A COLD. ACHOO!

Binoculars, joysticks, and cones add detail to a communications array

Colored stripes break up a plain hull

Tires prevent damage from bumping against docks and other boats

Robot claws and a flexible tube either side of the boat make great railings

Curved wall made with half arches

26

BOW BUILDING

Connecting sections of bricks with hinged bricks gives the boat its pointed bow. The forward deck is a wall built sideways from the body of the boat. Slopes help shape the deck so it fits into the angled curve of the hull.

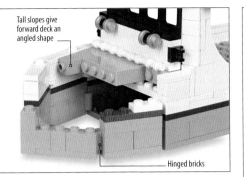

Tall slopes give forward deck an angled shape

Hinged bricks

BELOW DECK

If you're only building the part of the boat that sticks out of the water, not the whole thing, feel free to leave the bottom open—as long as the hull holds together!

Warning lights made by mounting transparent cones on poles

CRUISE CONTROL

A boat's control cabin is usually loaded with dials, levers, lights, radios, and receivers. Fill yours with as many technical-looking pieces as you can!

Working winch built with LEGO Technic pieces and a chain

You can't steer a boat without a rudder!

Fill barrels and crates with fish, crabs, clams... anything you like!

HOVER SCOOTER

When exploring alien worlds, your minifigure might need a small vehicle. But before you get building, ask yourself some simple questions. How will your vehicle travel? Does it roll on wheels, blast around with boosters, or zoom along on jet-powered sleds? What do you want your vehicle to do? It could explore space, build a space base...or even deliver pizza to a hungry rocket crew. Anything is possible!

KEEPIN' IT SMOOTH

If you have any curved pieces, try using them to give the front of your vehicle a sleek, aerodynamic profile. Contrasting colors look space-age and striking, especially red and black!

BUILDING BRIEF
Objective: Create space vehicles
Use: Exploration, transportation
Features: Must be able to hover
Extras: Radar, other comm devices

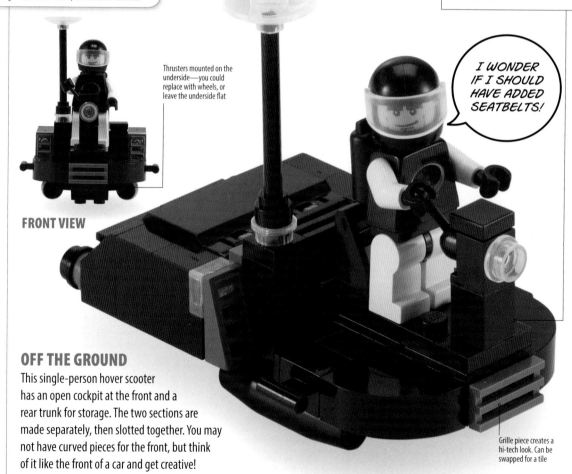

Transparent radar dish could be swapped for a flag or a lightbulb

Thrusters mounted on the underside—you could replace with wheels, or leave the underside flat

FRONT VIEW

I WONDER IF I SHOULD HAVE ADDED SEATBELTS!

Grille piece creates a hi-tech look. Can be swapped for a tile

OFF THE GROUND

This single-person hover scooter has an open cockpit at the front and a rear trunk for storage. The two sections are made separately, then slotted together. You may not have curved pieces for the front, but think of it like the front of a car and get creative!

Joystick allows minifigure pilot to steer the vehicle

SAFE STORAGE

Hinges are very useful pieces. On vehicles, you can use them to allow doors to open, wings to tilt upward or downward, or, as here, a trunk to open. Now just add your intergalactic cargo!

Don't have LEGO pizzas? Fill the trunk with tools, spare parts, or moon rocks

GUARANTEED DELIVERY IN 30 LIGHT-YEARS OR LESS!

Small rocket booster—or you could use this piece as a clip for wings

Red lights made from round transparent plates. Or you could use 1x1 cones or plates

NO STUDS IN SPACE

Using bricks with side studs or angle plates, you can build a section like this red side panel. Attach it sideways so none of the brick studs stick out.

You don't have to use a space-themed minifigure. Alien planets could have breathable atmospheres like Earth

REAR VIEW

SPACE WALKERS

Once you've arrived on a distant planet, your minifigures will want to explore! A walker is the perfect vehicle to scale alien terrain. Remember to build a stable, balanced walker: make sure the cockpit is not too big and heavy for the legs to support it.

BUILDING BRIEF

Objective: Create multi-legged space walkers
Use: Navigating across bumpy planet surfaces
Features: Jointed legs, swiveling cockpit
Extras: Radar, blasters for self-defense

ZZT QXT LKD
FFG KKOJH FJFJ! *

* TRANSLATION: IN THIS WALKER, SPACE CRATERS ARE SMALL FRY!

Just flick the robot missiles from the back with your finger to make them fire!

Robot missile launchers made from LEGO Technic beams with sticks

Using two 1x1 round plates to create an "ankle" is a simple way to add detail to your model

SIDE VIEW

REACHING THE TOP

You can connect the cockpit to the top of the legs using hinges and a flat 2x6 piece. If you have a turntable piece, you can make the cockpit swivel so the pilot can see all around.

SIMPLE WALKER

This simple walker model uses basic hinges to make the legs bend. If you haven't got any hinges, you could build even simpler, straight legs. How about adding a third leg, or even more?

Rocket thrusters attached with angle plate

Blasters could be replaced with wings; then the vehicle could walk...or fly!

Toes made from plates with bars. Think about how to use pieces in different ways!

REAR VIEW

ADVANCED WALKER

With more practice and pieces, you can build a walker with extra flexibility and details. Remember, the cockpit can be as simple or as complicated as you like, just so long as your minifigure can sit in it. Adding details, such as antennas, weapons, steering, and control panels, is the really fun bit!

RACE YOU TO THE NEAREST LUNAR COLONY!

Antennas are useful—these ones are creative—made from harpoon guns!

Blaster tips built from green transparent cones. Or you could use 1x1 round transparent pieces, radar dishes, or even loudhailer pieces!

Ball-and-socket joints help shape your walker's legs

Bars, antennas, and even screwdrivers can become rockets and blasters

Control panel made with a printed tile. A plain tile would work well, too

TOP VIEW

Some leg positions work better than others. See what's best for your model

REAR VIEW

BEST FOOT FORWARD

Look how easily you can make a cool foot with toes (for extra stability on rocky planet surfaces). 1x1 slopes form the toes, and they clip onto headlight bricks.

Headlight brick

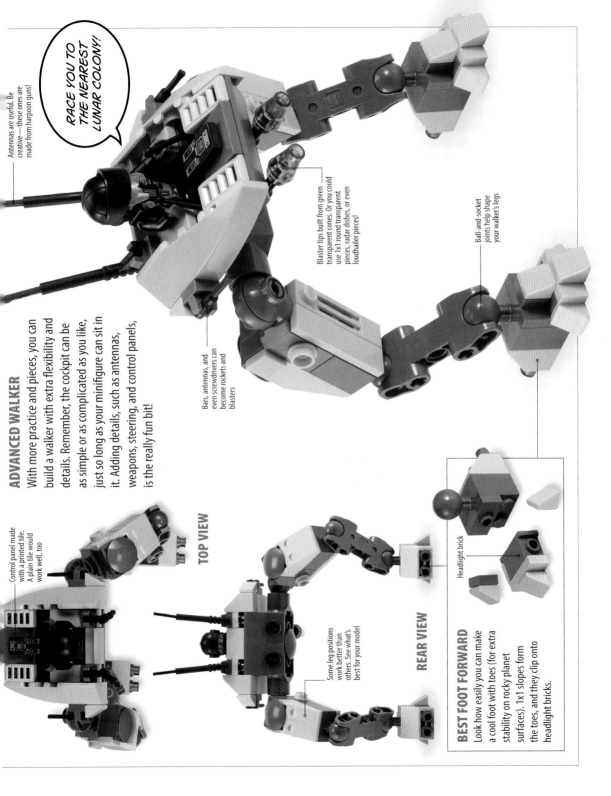

SMALL SPACESHIPS

All you need is a cockpit, some wings, and an engine or two, and you can build a small spaceship that's the perfect size for some serious outer-space adventure. Try to find pieces with unusual shapes to complete your build—and remember, there are no rules about what a spaceship should look like! Here are some ideas to get you started.

BUILDING BRIEF
Objective: Create small spaceships
Use: Space travel, adventure
Features: Lasers, tailfins, pilot controls
Types: Spacefighters, scouts, escape pods, racing ships

ADMIRAL'S INTERCEPTOR

The admiral flies his sleek interceptor into a space battle. The base of the ship is built with the studs facing upward, but the wings are built sideways, with the studs concealed. Landing skids, weapons, and a control pad add detail to the ship.

Choose a piece with an unusual shape to make a fancy tailfin

Curved slopes at the front lend a sleek and speedy look

Angled plates make the spaceship's outline look streamlined

You could add extra pieces to the tip to make a more powerful laser

Racing stripes made by placing plates between bricks of a contrasting color

ALTERNATIVE INTERCEPTOR

This simpler version of the interceptor has wings built with the studs facing up.

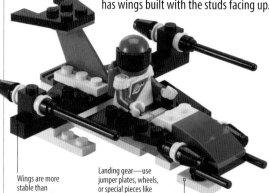

Wings are more stable than sideways-built wings

Landing gear—use jumper plates, wheels, or special pieces like minifigure skis

WINGING IT

To create smooth-looking wings, build two small stacks and turn them on their sides. Attach them to the core of the ship with angle plates. Use sloped or curved bricks to give your wings an exciting shape!

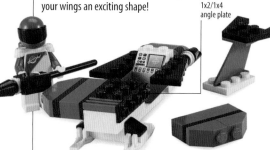

1x2/1x4 angle plate

ROCKET SHUTTLE MK I

This nippy little shuttle uses interesting looking pieces for texture, such as grille pieces, plates with bars, and a detailed slope as an engine. Using a plate with the studs facing up also adds to the functional look.

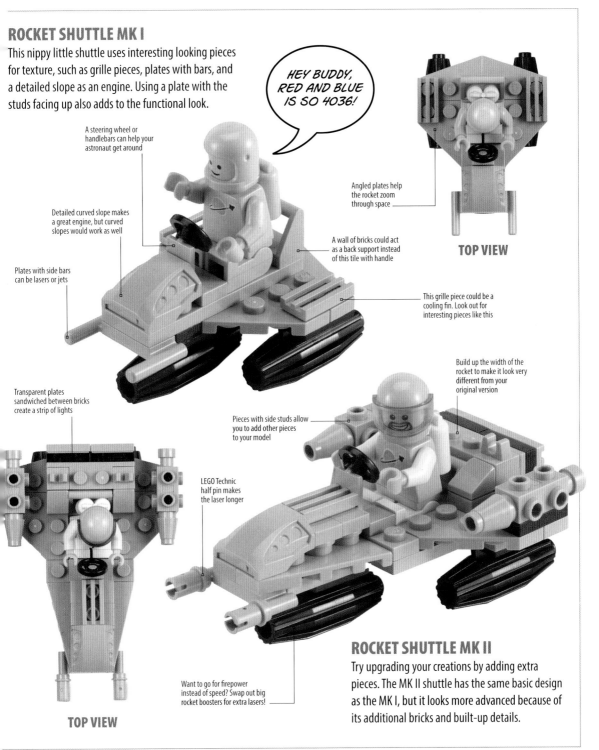

HEY BUDDY, RED AND BLUE IS SO 4036!

A steering wheel or handlebars can help your astronaut get around

Detailed curved slope makes a great engine, but curved slopes would work as well

Plates with side bars can be lasers or jets

Angled plates help the rocket zoom through space

TOP VIEW

A wall of bricks could act as a back support instead of this tile with handle

This grille piece could be a cooling fin. Look out for interesting pieces like this

Transparent plates sandwiched between bricks create a strip of lights

Pieces with side studs allow you to add other pieces to your model

Build up the width of the rocket to make it look very different from your original version

LEGO Technic half pin makes the laser longer

Want to go for firepower instead of speed? Swap out big rocket boosters for extra lasers!

TOP VIEW

ROCKET SHUTTLE MK II

Try upgrading your creations by adding extra pieces. The MK II shuttle has the same basic design as the MK I, but it looks more advanced because of its additional bricks and built-up details.

MORE SMALL SPACESHIPS

There are so many ways to build small space vehicles. You could try grabbing a random handful of pieces and seeing what you can make. You might be amazed! Or look around you at the shapes of everyday objects. They could inspire your creations. Now, get building!

Base made of plates

Headlight brick

SEPARATE SIDES

The sides are built separately and attached side-on to two headlight bricks on each side of the ship body

I LOVE FEELING THE SOLAR WIND BLOWING MY TENTACLES!

PURPLE PATROLLER

Guess what inspired this small patroller vehicle? A highlighter! The ship is built around a 2x8 plate with purple curved pieces for sides. The highlighter tip could be a sensor device—or maybe it emits a glowing beam!

These purple gr[...] make great eng[...] cooling vents

1x2 brick with side studs

Front is made from black and green plates and slopes, and attached side-on to a brick with side studs

Even aliens need to get around!

Side details made from a 1x2 jumper plate and two black 1x1 round plates

Blue transparent piece peeps through the grille

Front lights created with a 2x3 curved plate with hole, behind which is a blue transparent piece

Joystick controls, but you could use a steering wheel or handlebars

Exhaust vent made from a transparent 1x2 grille attached side-on to two headlight bricks at the rear

REAR VIEW

SIDE VIEW

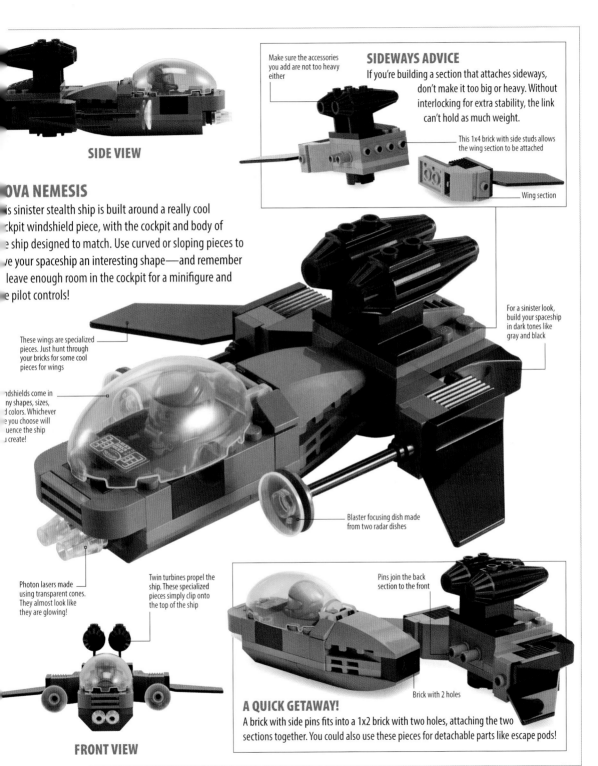

SIDE VIEW

Make sure the accessories you add are not too heavy either

SIDEWAYS ADVICE

If you're building a section that attaches sideways, don't make it too big or heavy. Without interlocking for extra stability, the link can't hold as much weight.

This 1x4 brick with side studs allows the wing section to be attached

Wing section

OVA NEMESIS

s sinister stealth ship is built around a really cool ckpit windshield piece, with the cockpit and body of e ship designed to match. Use curved or sloping pieces to ve your spaceship an interesting shape—and remember leave enough room in the cockpit for a minifigure and e pilot controls!

These wings are specialized pieces. Just hunt through your bricks for some cool pieces for wings

ndshields come in ny shapes, sizes, d colors. Whichever e you choose will uence the ship u create!

For a sinister look, build your spaceship in dark tones like gray and black

Blaster focusing dish made from two radar dishes

Photon lasers made using transparent cones. They almost look like they are glowing!

Twin turbines propel the ship. These specialized pieces simply clip onto the top of the ship

Pins join the back section to the front

Brick with 2 holes

A QUICK GETAWAY!

A brick with side pins fits into a 1x2 brick with two holes, attaching the two sections together. You could also use these pieces for detachable parts like escape pods!

FRONT VIEW

MICROSHIPS

You may not have a lot of bricks to build with. Or perhaps the space model you want to make would be too complicated at minifigure scale. Or maybe you want a whole fleet of ships for a big space battle. Why not try microbuilding? It is exactly like regular minifigure-scale building but on a smaller scale, and you can assemble some of the coolest—and smallest—spaceships around!

BUILDING WITH HOLES
You'll find that some pieces have holes in them, such as this 1x2 brick with cross axle hole. They are just the right size to grip blasters, antennas, and other accessories.

BUILDING BRIEF
Objective: Build microscale spaceships
Use: Everything a big spaceship does...only smaller!
Features: Must have recognizable spaceship features
Extras: Escort fighters, motherships, space bases

Radio antennas built from accessories like harpoon guns or telescopes

Use antennas, lances, or blasters as weapons

Hinged plates

Microcockpit—use transparent pieces, solid sloped pieces, or even two contrasting 1x1 pieces

Laser weapons—neon transparent pieces look hi-tech

BUTTERFLY SHUTTLE
The wings and body of this microship were built separately, then attached together. The wings are connected to each other with hinged plates, allowing you to fold them at any angle you choose before clipping them onto the main body.

In microscale, a single engine piece can become an entire spaceship body

Lights match the cockpit windshield here—but they can be any color!

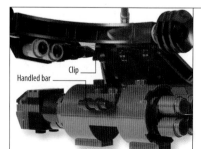

Clip

Handled bar

CLIP-ON WINGS
The wings are built with clips on the underside. These snap onto bars sticking out of the side of the ship's body. It can be tricky to attach the wings, but once they are in place they will look like they are floating!

SIDE VIEW

SPACE HAULER

This Space Hauler transports heavy freight across the galaxy. Round barrels full of cargo clip onto the main body of the hauler. The barrels have been unloaded and replaced so many times, it's no wonder they don't match!

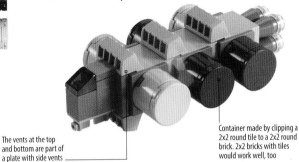

Angle plates

TOP VIEW

The vents at the top and bottom are part of a plate with side vents

Container made by clipping a 2x2 round tile to a 2x2 round brick. 2x2 bricks with tiles would work well, too

CARGO COLUMN

The core of the Space Hauler is a simple column of bricks and plates turned on its side. Angle plates form attachment points for the cargo containers.

Brick with side studs

INNER WORKINGS

A simple exterior can conceal clever building techniques inside. Here, bricks with side studs support the white curved slopes, and LEGO Technic half pins hold the top and bottom dishes together.

A group of identical flying saucers with different-colored parts could be a microscale invasion fleet!

FLYING SAUCER

Sometimes you have a piece that you just know would look great as part of a microship. The design of this classic UFO is inspired by a pair of big, orange radar dishes.

Flight wing made from two flag pieces. Rudder pieces would give a similar effect

Central ring made of curved slopes attached together to form a circle

Radar dish pieces can be engines, cockpits, transmitters, or even landing gear!

TOP VIEW

SHUTTLE AND ESCORTS

For an extra challenge, build a microscale spaceship and then make some even tinier escort vehicles with matching designs to protect it on its interstellar missions!

Jets or thrusters can be made from chrome pieces, like these LEGO® Star Wars® lightsaber hilts

MORE MICROSHIPS

The design of your microship should say as much as possible about its purpose and function. Is your mission one of peaceful exploration? Galactic adventure? Combat and conquest? Think carefully about which pieces will best tell the story—because it only takes a few bricks to build a whole ship!

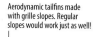

Aerodynamic tailfins made with grille slopes. Regular slopes would work just as well!

Drone escorts protect the stellar explorer!

This piece can be found in LEGO® Games sets. You could also use a 1x1 cone

STELLAR EXPLORER

This microship may be small, but its design is actually quite complex. Its bricks face in four different directions: up, down, left, and right! Use a central column of bricks with side studs as your starting point. It may take some time to achieve a smooth, sleek look!

Exhaust nozzles made from two radar dishes in contrasting colors

Thrusters made from LEGO Technic T-bars plugged into a 1x1 brick with 4 side studs

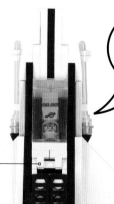

THIS COCKPIT'S A PERFECT FIT! BLAST OFF!

Windshield attached to the tail by a clip and bar hinge, so it can open and close

Rudder piece is a good size for a microship wing. You could also use flag pieces, or build wings of different shapes!

TOP VIEW

Think these engines are too small? Replace them with one giant engine!

REAR VIEW

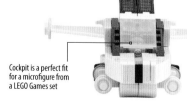

Cockpit is a perfect fit for a microfigure from a LEGO Games set

FRONT VIEW

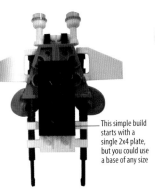

This simple build starts with a single 2x4 plate, but you could use a base of any size

BOTTOM VIEW

SIDE VIEW

STAR CARRIER

The Star Carrier is quite a basic build, but it transports troops and battle vehicles across the galaxy! Plates with horizontal clips hold weapons in place and tiles give a smooth finish.

APPROACHING TARGET FOR OPERATION MICRO!

Harpoon gun is a novel way to attach a radar dish

LEADING THE WAY

A slide plate forms a battering ram at the front—and hides the hollow bottom of the stack. Alternatively, you could use an inverted slope piece to give your cruiser a wedge-nosed shape.

1x1 round plate can be used to dock the microship onto a space station

Engine housings made from LEGO Technic beams with sticks. Swap the transparent pieces for flick-fire space torpedoes!

BATTLE CRUISER

This sturdy, menacing ship is on a mission to smash other microships to smithereens! The battle cruiser is built as a stack of bricks and then turned on its side.

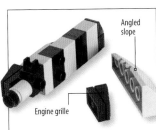

Angled slope

Engine grille

BUILDING SECRETS

Bricks with side studs hold the angled slopes and engine grilles in place. Transparent red pieces under the grille slopes make it look like energy is glowing through the vents.

SPACE AMBASSADOR

Friendly colors and curves, and the absence of weaponry, make this spaceship look like it belongs to a peaceful species. This microship is quite simple to build, but there are lots of areas where detail has been added.

Microcockpit made with 1x1 slope. You could also use a 1x1 plate or a grille piece for an armored cockpit!

Tailfins—this clip could also hold extra weapons, equipment, or even a detachable mini-microship

MEET THE BUILDER

BARNEY MAIN

Location: UK
Age: 18
LEGO Specialty: Pirates, transport

How old were you when you started using LEGO bricks?

I was 18 months old when I got my first LEGO® DUPLO® set, but moved on to LEGO sets shortly afterward—and haven't stopped since then!

Which model were you most proud of as a young LEGO builder?

A model of a Viking warrior's head called "Infuriated Isaac" that I built when I was nine years old. It was featured in the *LEGO® Magazine*, as "Designer's Choice," which I was very proud of!

This pirate ship flies through the skies, catching lightning using the nets on the back. It was inspired by the movie *Stardust*, but I added a whole load of my own ideas, such as the lightning-sharks!

Both the blades of the windmill and the wooden boarding on the sides are made by "stepping" plates, and putting tiles on top. It's a very versatile technique, and has a lot of applications.

What are you inspired by?

Anything and everything! The basic idea for a model stems from all sorts of things—discovering a cool part combination, films and literature, or seeing something in real life. Often I see something that I'd like to replicate, such as a style of stonework, but only recall it a couple of months later when I'm building and decide to put it in! Sometimes if I'm entering a contest with a specific theme, I do my research more thoroughly: I once had to build a model of my own Dr. Seuss story, so I read through a lot of his books again to get the style right. That said, my finished models rarely look anything like my initial idea—I just go with the flow, really, and let the model itself dictate how it's going to look!

What is the biggest or most complex model you've made?

I built a big battle scene from the movie *The Chronicles of Narnia: Prince Caspian*. The battlefield was actually raised off the ground so that I could build the tomb inside the mountain, and also the sink-hole that opens up in the ground in the movie. It was really fun making all the Narnian mythical creatures—griffins, centaurs, satyrs—as well as making the famous cracked Stone Table and the siege weapons.

If you had all the LEGO bricks (and time!) in the world, what would you build?

That's a tough one. I enjoy building at real-life scale, so maybe something like a full-size version of myself! I'm also a big fan of the musical *Les Misérables* and would like to do a large, detailed version of the iconic barricade scene.

Models that use only a few colors can look really stylish, but multicolored models are fun, too!

Condensing the various scenes from Charles Dickens' *A Christmas Carol* into one model was a big challenge, as was capturing the characters in minifigure form! Lots of different colors and textures are used to help differentiate the different scenes, and the roof is made out of diving flippers!

The water here is built by turning a wall on its side to get a nice smooth surface. I left holes where I wanted the boats to go. There are loads of different parts supporting the inside of the cliff—pillars, castle towers, LEGO Technic bricks, and so on—but you can't see them!

What is your favorite creation?

I really like my life-size version of the Three Blind Mice from the nursery rhyme. I think I captured the mice's expressions, the carving knife, and all the gory details really well! The cheese was made from Modulex, which is a miniature LEGO brick from the 1960s used for architectural modeling!

What are some of your top LEGO tips?

Brick separators are incredibly useful! I have three lying around in case of an emergency, and it saves having to bite the bricks or ruin your fingernails. As for building, just use what bricks you have, and be creative! Think about what parts you have a lot of—if you've got lots of green bricks, why not make a giant frog? Or if you've got lots of white horns, how about a dragon, using the horns for its spine?

How much time do you spend building?

Normally an hour or two a day.

Although this pirate hideout was designed as a static display scene, it's useful to think about the backstory: Why is the soldier being made to walk the plank? Who hid all the treasure here? Why are the pirates battling each other?

What is your favorite LEGO technique or technique you use the most?

I love coming up with innovative ways to make roofing. For example, diving flippers make a great-looking Gothic tiled roof. I bought 250 black flippers specifically for this!

How many LEGO bricks do you have?

Not enough! At the last count, around 15,000 pieces (although that was a fair few years back).

I JUST GO WITH THE FLOW, REALLY, AND LET THE MODEL ITSELF DICTATE HOW IT'S GOING TO LOOK!

Designer's Choice

"Infuriated Isaac"
Barney Main, 9

Building a head is quite similar to building the hot air balloon on p.30, but with added details and facial features. The key to a character is often getting detail around the eyes right—Infuriated Isaac has a very shifty expression!

The big challenge for this castle was the steep grassy slopes up to the keep, which were done using hinged bricks and plates. The battlements have some intricate detailing, and the castle even has its own toilet!

What things have gone wrong and how have you dealt with them?

Something I find challenging is being color-blind. It can be very difficult to distinguish colors, and I have no concept of whether they clash or not. Also, only having a student budget, I don't have nearly the amount of bricks I'd like. I frequently have to make compromises with the size and color of models, which is why there's normally a lot of gray in them! However, not having enough bricks can be beneficial, as it forces you to innovate and come up with new ways of doing things.

What is your favorite LEGO brick or piece?

That's tricky! There are a lot of parts that I invariably use, but I'll have to go with the headlight brick. It's really useful for turning bricks on their sides or upside down, and you can attach both bricks and bars to it. But be warned—it is actually slightly thicker than a brick, as the stud on the side sticks out a bit, and this can make building with it tricky sometimes.

What do you enjoy building the most?

I don't normally build transport, so this project was venturing into new territory for me. I love pirates and castles—but anything that is green, brown, gray, and gritty suits my taste. Urban streets are also fun to do, as there's so much scope for color and texture. I'd like to get good at making spaceships, but find them really difficult to build, as I always want to add sails or battlements!

Do you plan out your build? If so, how?

Not really! I sometimes do a rough sketch but generally I just start building and hope it goes to plan! I tend to think about the next step in a model when I'm not building, and I've been known to wake up during the night with an idea what to do next! Naturally, I implement it immediately...

Minifigures really bring a model to life! You don't even have to put in the whole minifigure—look at the man hiding in a floating barrel!

This museum is compatible with LEGO® Modular Buildings, such as Café Corner. It is, however, considerably more dilapidated, with its broken windows and grimy streets.

You can build things that you see around you, things that you may only have seen in books or photographs—like this swampboat—or creations that come entirely from your imagination!

MEET THE BUILDER

TIM GODDARD

Location: UK
Age: 34
LEGO Specialty: Microscale space

What are some of your top LEGO tips?

Use SNOT a lot! This is a term that LEGO fans use, it stands for Studs Not On Top and means that you don't just build with the brick studs pointing up. There are loads of interesting bricks that have studs on the side that can be used for this. Another tip is to sort out the bricks in your collection a bit. It may seem like it takes a lot of time, but it can save you time in the long run, as you know just where that brick you need is stored!

This shows the hangar area and part of a road system on a recently settled alien world. This is only part of a large display that was built as a collaboration with another LEGO builder, Peter Reid.

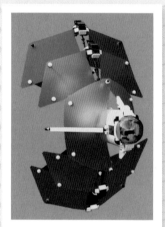

This research craft studies stars in far-off systems. It uses giant solar sails to power its scientific equipment and its engines.

This is the headquarters of the space police. It can communicate over vast distances and is used by commanders to meet up and discuss what the evil aliens have been up to.

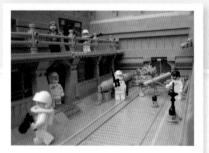

Inside a federation outpost a worker discovers one of the fiber optical cables has been damaged. Did it break or was it sabotage?

How much time do you spend building?

It probably averages out at about an hour a day. I don't always have time but I find late in the evening is the best time for inspiration, while playing my favorite music.

THE BEST THING TO DO WITH LARGER MODELS IS PLAN AHEAD.

What things have gone wrong and how have you dealt with them?

Larger models, such as big spaceships, can be a bit unstable. This is especially a problem when I concentrate more on the detail and shape above the structure of the model. The best thing to do with larger models is plan ahead—build a nice solid frame then add the fancy stuff on top.

What is your favorite creation?

The one I'm working on at the moment! I do like the models that I've made to have a bit of character to them, such as a giraffe I've finished recently. Even robots can have a bit of character—building so you can tilt the head a bit to one side or have the arms in expressive positions is really satisfying.

Outside an alien nightclub the space police catch up with a wanted fugitive, but not before he has caused some chaos!

What is the biggest or most complex model you've made?

The largest things I have built have been a couple of small-scale *Star Wars* dioramas (scenes). I have built a couple about 1.5m by 0.75m (12ft 11in by 2ft 6in) filled with lots of small ships and walkers. The great thing about large scenes is you can gradually build and design the small craft and then make landscape, plants, and buildings and gradually add to the whole display. When it is all put together you end up with a great, entirely LEGO environment.

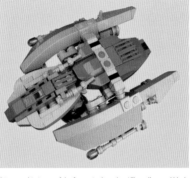

This spaceship is one of the fastest in the galaxy! The yellow and black markings are called bumblebee stripes.

This cargo hauler is specially adapted to travel over bumpy lunar terrain. It has room for one minifigure astronaut

How old were you when you started using LEGO bricks?

I've been building for as long as I can remember! I must have been four or five when I started building.

Do you plan out your build? If so, how?

It depends on what I'm building: I just tend to go for it with smaller models but larger models need a bit more planning. I sometimes sketch out the shape of a spaceship or the layout of a diorama but never in too much detail. I often have an idea of a particular little bit of design—like a wing shape—and just build what I think looks good with it. I carry on designing as I build, seeing what I think looks good as well as using the bricks I have available.

If you had all the LEGO bricks (and tim in the world, what would you build?

A really big space display that has lots of minifigures and spaceships, with lots of moving parts and brick-built landscapi and a large moon base with loads of internal detail. I would also like to build a what LEGO fans call a SHIP (Seriously Heavy Investment in Parts) of original design, maybe that could land at the moon base above! But these big ideas don't mean I don't enjoy building little models that can fit in your hand.

This powerful ship uses a neutralizing weapon to catch unsuspecting transport spaceships.

A small submarine discovers some underwater ruins. Could this be the remains of the lost city of Atlantis?

This green space walker, with coordinating green alien minifigure, would be hard to spot on a jungle planet!

How many LEGO bricks do you have?

I have no idea! Lots and lots, but I never seem to have the bit that I'm looking for!

What are you inspired by?

[A]ll sorts of things: sci-fi films and TV programs, buildings and [sc]enery I see when I am driving around, old LEGO® Space sets. [B]ut the thing that inspires me to build interesting things more [th]an anything else is seeing other people's LEGO creations.

What is your favorite LEGO technique [o]r the technique you use the most?

[S]NOT is a real favorite and I use it all the time. I also enjoy [c]ombining pieces with clips and bars—it's great for [m]aking robots!

What types of models do you enjoy making, apart from space?

I enjoy building everything and anything in LEGO bricks! I like building animals—I've built a giraffe and some hippos. I also like town buildings and anything that involves minifigures. I think the more different things and areas you build in, the better you get as you discover new techniques.

At the robotics development facility the professor of robotics introduces his latest creation to the senior spacemen. The new robot will help around the base, carrying out various maintenance duties.

[A] trio of aliens are ready to take on the space police. Aliens of all shapes and [size]s are welcome here, as long as they are bad!

This dinosaur-style mechanical transport is used to traverse treacherous, unexplored planets. It has room for one minifigure pilot to sit in the head section.

What is your favorite LEGO brick or piece?

[T]he standard 2x4 LEGO brick is a real classic, but I [t]hink the piece I use the most is a 1x1 plate with [s]ide ring. You can do so many things with it!

Which model were you most proud of as a young LEGO builder?

[A]s I was growing up I had a lot of the LEGO Space sets. I made my bedroom into a giant alien [p]lanet and had different settlements around the room, one on a shelf and one on a chest of [d]rawers, and had spaceships hanging from the ceiling flying between them. So I suppose [t]he answer is not just one model but a whole series that made up my own world!

I'VE BEEN BUILDING FOR AS LONG AS I CAN REMEMBER!

DK

LONDON, NEW YORK
MELBOURNE, MUNICH, and DEHLI

Editor Shari Last
Additional Editors Simon Beecroft, Jo Casey, Hannah Dolan,
Emma Grange, Catherine Saunders, Lisa Stock, Victoria Taylor
Senior Editor Laura Gilbert
Designer Owen Bennett
Additional Designers Guy Harvey, Lynne Moulding, Robert Perry,
Lisa Sodeau, Ron Stobbart, Rhys Thomas, Toby Truphet
Senior Designer Nathan Martin
Design Manager Ron Stobbart
Art Director Lisa Lanzarini
Publishing Manager Catherine Saunders
Publisher Simon Beecroft
Publishing Director Alex Allan
Production Editor Sean Daly
Production Controller Nick Seston

Photography by Gary Ombler,
Brian Poulsen, and Tim Trøjborg

This American Edition published in 2013
Contains content previously published in the United States in 2011 in
The LEGO® Ideas Book
001-194846 Sep/13

Published in the United States by DK Publishing
345 Hudson Street, New York, New York 10014

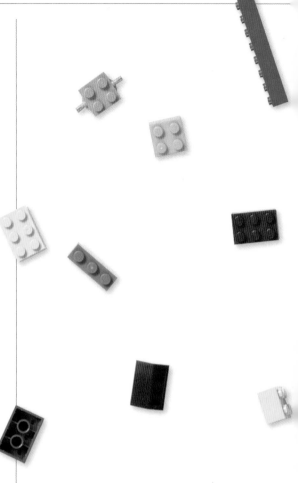

DK books are available at special discounts when purchased in bulk for sales promotions,
premiums, fund-raising, or educational use. For details, contact: DK Publishing Special
Markets, 375 Hudson Street, New York, New York 100014specialsales@dk.com.

A catalog record for this book is available from the Library of Congress.
ISBN: 978-1-4654-1366-6

Reproduced by MDP in the UK
Printed and bound in China by Leo Paper Products Ltd.

Discover more at
www.dk.com
www.LEGO.com

Acknowledgments

Dorling Kindersley would like to thank: Stephanie Lawrence,
Randi Sørensen, and Corinna van Delden at the LEGO Group;
Tim Goddard and Barney Main for their amazing models; Jeff van
Winden for additional building; Daniel Lipkowitz for his fantastic
text; Gary Ombler, Brian Poulsen, and Tim Trøjborg for their
brilliant photography; Rachel Peng and Bo Wei at IM Studios;
and Sarah Harland for editorial assistance.